Dragsters

By Kathleen W. Deady

Consultants:
The staff of
The Museum of Drag Racing
Ocala, Florida

CAPSTONE
HIGH-INTEREST
BOOKS

an imprint of Capstone Press
Mankato, Minnesota

Capstone High-Interest Books are published by Capstone Press
151 Good Counsel Drive, P.O. Box 669, Mankato, Minnesota 56002
http://www.capstone-press.com

Library of Congress Cataloging-in-Publication Data
Deady, Kathleen W.
    Dragsters/by Kathleen W. Deady.
    p. cm.—(Wild rides)
    Includes bibliographical references and index.
    ISBN 0-7368-0926-0
    1. Dragsters—Juvenile literature. [1. Drag racing. 2. Automobiles, Racing.]
I. Title. II. Series.
TL236.2 .D43 2002
629.228—dc21   2001000209

Summary: Discusses these fast race cars, their history, parts, and competitions.

Editorial Credits
Matt Doeden, editor; Karen Risch, product planning editor, Kia Bielke,
    cover and interior designer; Katy Kudela, photo researcher

Photo Credits
ALLSPORT PHOTOGRAPHY, cover, 8, 25
Isaac Hernandez/Mercury Press, 6, 24, 27
Louise Ann Noeth, 13, 14, 28
Photo Network/Mark Sherman, 20–21
SportsChrome-USA/Rob Tringali Jr., 4, 7, 16, 22
Unicorn Stock Photos/H. Schmeiser, 10

The author wishes to thank Ron Gagnon at the New England Rod Shop for his
assistance in preparing this book.

1 2 3 4 5 6 07 06 05 04 03 02

Table of Contents

Learn about:

- **Dragster races**

- **Cost of dragsters**

- **Dragster classes**

CHAPTER 1

Dragsters

Two drivers rev their engines at the starting line. The engines roar as the drivers prepare to start the race.

The green starting light flashes. Thick clouds of smoke fill the air as the drivers begin the race. The cars speed down the straight track. They cross the finish line after only a few seconds. But they have traveled about one-fourth mile (402 meters).

The drivers are racing cars called dragsters. These cars have powerful supercharged engines. They are the fastest race cars in the world.

People build dragsters for instant power and speed.

About Dragsters

People build dragsters for instant power and speed. The cars travel more than 300 miles (483 kilometers) per hour. They must be able to gain speed quickly. Dragsters can accelerate to their top speeds in only a few seconds.

People drive dragsters in drag races. Only two drivers take part in each race. These races are called eliminations. The dragsters start side by side. On a signal, drivers accelerate as fast as they can. The first driver across the finish line wins the elimination.

The fastest dragster does not always win the race. Drivers must get a quick start. They try to get off the starting line before their opponent does. Even the smallest head start can make the difference in such a short race.

Dragsters are very expensive to build and race. Top cars can cost more than $100,000 to build. A dragster's high speeds are hard on its engine. A driver can use an engine only once. The race team must rebuild it after every race. The new engine parts may cost more than $3,000. Fuel for a single race may cost $400 or more.

Pro stockers are drag racing cars built from standard cars.

Funny cars have no doors, no trunk, and no hood.

Dragster Classes

People race different types of drag racing cars. Racing officials group cars into classes based on their features. These include engine size, weight, and the kind of fuel they use. Some drag races are held for trucks or motorcycles. But most drag races feature cars.

There are three professional classes of drag racing cars. They are dragsters, funny cars, and pro stockers. Professional drivers earn money by taking part in races in these classes.

Dragsters are the fastest drag racing cars. They sometimes are called "top fuelers." Dragsters are nearly 25 feet (7.6 meters) long. This length is about twice the length of most cars. They also are very narrow and low to the ground. A top fueler is about 3 feet (.9 meter) wide and 3 feet high.

Funny cars look like standard cars. But a funny car's body has no doors, no trunk, and no hood. Instead, the outside shell of the car lifts up from the front. Funny cars also have large rear tires. These tires cause the back end to sit high off the ground.

Pro stockers are built from standard cars. Drivers modify these cars. They change the engines to make the cars more powerful.

Learn about:

- **Hot rods**

- **Early dragsters**

- **Don Garlits**

CHAPTER 2

Early Models of Dragsters

Automobile racing first became popular during the 1920s and 1930s. A popular model of car at this time was the Model T Ford. This car also was a popular race car.

People wanted the fastest, most powerful cars for racing. They modified their cars. They made small changes to their cars to improve speed and performance. Some people called these modified cars "hot rods."

Hot rods were popular during the 1930s and 1940s. Many racers bought classic cars such as Model T Fords. The racers turned the cars into hot rods. They then raced the cars. Most of these cars could reach speeds of more than 90 miles (145 kilometers) per hour. But there were no rules for building hot rods. There also were no rules for racing them.

Early Dragsters

The National Hot Rod Association (NHRA) formed in the 1950s. This group organized the sport and set racing guidelines. One set of rules was for drag racing. Cars that took part in drag races soon were called dragsters.

Major manufacturers such as General Motors worked to build better engines. Individual racers also tried new designs. Some tried using two separate engines in one car. Others tried to use airplane engines in cars. Racers also tried using different kinds of fuel to power these engines.

Racers also continued to improve the body design of their cars. They removed unnecessary parts such as headlights and fenders. These changes made the cars faster and more lightweight. Racers also tried new tires that could better handle fast acceleration.

All of these changes resulted in faster dragsters. In 1957, racer Don Garlits set a record of 156.5 miles (252 kilometers) per hour.

Garlits remained one of the most famous drag racers during the 1960s and 1970s. He was the first driver to reach speeds of 200 miles (322 kilometers) per hour and 250 miles (402 kilometers) per hour.

Don Garlits was one of drag racing's first stars.

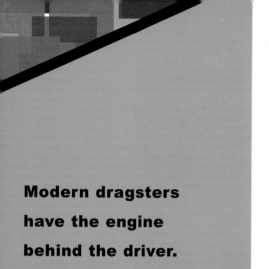

Modern dragsters have the engine behind the driver.

Major Advances

Garlits advanced the sport of drag racing in many ways. His inventions were designed to increase dragsters' speed. For example, he used sticky tires that gave him a faster start.

He also developed the rear engine dragster. This dragster's engine was located behind the driver. This new design was safer for drivers. Engine fires did not travel back toward the driver.

Garlits also was the first racer to use an air spoiler on a dragster's front end. A spoiler is shaped like an airplane wing. It helps keep the car steady and on the race track.

Recent Advancements

By the late 1970s, the NHRA had seven different car classes. At first, dragsters were the most popular. But funny cars later became the most popular class. One famous funny car driver was named Kenny Bernstein. In 1992, Bernstein became the first racer to reach a speed of 300 miles (483 kilometers) per hour.

Today, racers continue to improve dragsters. They use computers to test new designs and models. They also use computers to make sure that engines are running at the highest level. In 1999, these improvements helped racer Tony Schumacher reach 330 miles (531 kilometers) per hour.

Learn about:

- **Aerodynamics**

- **Engines**

- **Tires**

CHAPTER **3**

Designing a Dragster

Dragsters must move smoothly through air. Air must easily flow around and past the cars. Air that does not easily flow around dragsters causes resistance. Air resistance slows down dragsters.

Engineers study different body designs that may reduce air resistance. These designs are aerodynamic. Dragsters with aerodynamic body designs can reach the highest possible speeds. Aerodynamic dragsters are smooth and rounded. They have no flat surfaces that could trap air.

Aerodynamics is not the only important part of body design. Air flows under a dragster as it travels. At high speeds, this air can lift the dragster off the ground. Engineers must build a dragster's body very close to the ground. This design allows less air to flow under the car.

Dragsters also have wheelie bars. These small extra wheels stick out behind the car. They prevent the front end from lifting. Wheelie bars keep dragsters from flipping at high speeds.

Engines

Dragsters have internal combustion engines. This type of engine includes several cylinders. Fuel burns inside these pipe-shaped chambers.

Many dragsters have special fuel systems. A fuel injection system forces fuel quickly into the cylinders. This system gives the dragster steady power. Some dragster engines have blowers to force air into the cylinders. The air helps the fuel burn quickly. Cars with blowers are called "supercharged." Supercharged cars have increased acceleration.

Many dragsters burn gasoline. But some use nitromethane. People call this fuel "nitro" for short. Nitro is a mix of nitric acid and propane gas. It gives engines extra power. Some dragsters use alcohol as fuel. Alcohol also increases engine power.

People measure engine power in horsepower. Engines in normal cars produce about 150 horsepower. Dragster engines may produce 6,000 horsepower or more.

Turbocharger

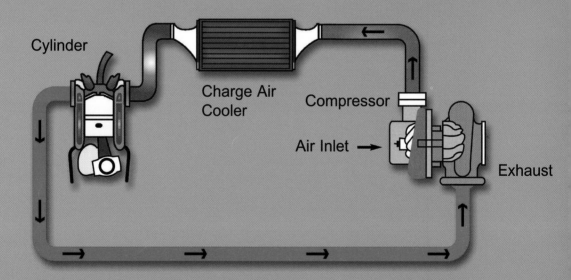

Turbochargers work by pumping extra air into the cylinder. This air allows the cylinder to burn more fuel. Air enters a turbocharger through an inlet. The air then goes through a compressor. The compressor sends the air to a charge air cooler. The charge air cooler cools the air and sends it to the cylinder. The cylinder heats the air as it burns fuel. The heated air then travels back through an air flow to an exhaust discharge. The air leaves the system through this outlet.

Starting and Stopping

Acceleration is one of the most important dragster features. Drivers must get a fast start to win an elimination. Their tires need to grip the pavement tightly. This grip is called traction.

Racers use tires called slicks on the rear wheels. Slicks are about 3 feet (.9 meter) high and 1.5 feet (.5 meter) wide. They are made of soft, sticky rubber. Dragster tires are smooth. They do not have tread to help them grip the track. Racers spin their tires to heat the rubber before they start. The heat makes the rubber sticky and gives the tires good traction.

Some dragsters such as top fuelers include an airfoil. This device is attached to the back of the car. An airfoil works like an airplane wing. But it causes air to force the car down instead of up. This downward force presses the tires more tightly to the ground. It gives them better traction.

Most dragsters travel so fast that they need help to slow down. Many dragsters carry a parachute mounted behind the driver. The driver pulls a cord to open the parachute. The parachute opens behind the car. It causes enough air resistance to slow down the car.

Some dragsters have parachutes to help them slow down.

Learn

about:

- **The strip**

- **Events**

- **Safety**

CHAPTER 4

Dragsters in Competition

The early years of drag racing were not organized. People raced on city streets and on straight country roads. Some even raced on dry riverbeds. Races seldom had set rules. The cars often were unevenly matched.

People began to organize the sport in the 1930s and 1940s. Many small racing clubs formed in the United States and Canada. These clubs organized and held races. Today, organizations such as the NHRA set rules and standards for drag races. These standards help to keep the sport safe and fair.

A "Christmas tree" is a pole with colored lights. The lights tell drivers when a race will begin.

PRE-STAGE

STAGE

NHRA

The Modern Drag Race

Today, drag races take place on a track called a strip. The strip is made of asphalt. This paved surface is smooth and even. Most drag races are 1,320 feet (402 meters) long. This distance is about one-fourth mile. Some races are only 660 feet (201 meters) long. This distance is about one-eighth mile.

A drag racing strip is longer than one-fourth mile. It continues beyond the finish line. The part of the strip past the finish line is called the shutdown strip. Drivers use this part of the strip to slow down and stop.

Events

Many dragster teams begin each event. Two dragsters run in each elimination. The losing driver can no longer race in the event.

The drivers begin at the starting line. A pole with colored lights tells drivers when to begin the race. This pole is called a Christmas tree because of its red and green lights. Drivers race to the finish line once the green light comes on.

Winning drivers advance to the next round of competition. They continue with eliminations until only two drivers remain. The winner of the final race is called the top eliminator.

Drag races take place on a long track called a strip.

Safety

Drag racing can be dangerous. At high speeds, small problems with a car or track can be deadly. Officials inspect dragsters before a race. They check that all parts are working properly and are in good condition. They weigh the car to be sure that it meets the requirements for its class. They also check for additional safety equipment.

Dragsters sometimes catch fire during races. Drivers wear suits made of materials that do not burn or melt in a fire. Even their socks, gloves, shoes, and underwear must be fireproof. Drivers also carry a fire extinguisher inside the car. They use it to put out any fires that start before or after a race.

Dragsters must have a roll bar or roll cage. This frame is made of steel pipes. These strong pipes surround the driver. They protect the driver if the car rolls over.

Dragsters also must have safety harnesses. These seat belts hold the driver in place. They prevent the driver from being thrown from the car during a crash.

Drivers wear helmets and fire suits
for safety.

Kenny Bernstein

Kenny Bernstein was born September 6, 1944. He began racing in 1966 as a hobby. He was a skilled racer. He won many of the events he entered.

Bernstein raced funny cars. He quickly became one of the best drivers in the world. In 1973, he reached the NHRA funny car finals. He won the funny car championship four years in a row from 1985 to 1988.

In 1990, Bernstein began racing top fuelers. In 1992, he became the first person to race 300 miles (483 kilometers) per hour in a dragster. People call Bernstein "The King of Speed" for his accomplishments.

Words to Know

accelerate (ak-SEL-uh-rate)—to gain speed

aerodynamic (air-oh-dye-NAM-mik)—designed to reduce air resistance

airfoil (AIR-foil)—a winglike feature attached to the back of a dragster to push the back end down

asphalt (ASS-fawlt)—a smooth, even pavement used on drag racing strips

cylinder (SIL-uhn-dur)—a hollow chamber inside an engine in which fuel is burned to create power

elimination (ee-lim-uh-NAY-shuhn)—a drag race including two cars

fiberglass (FYE-bur-glass)—a strong, lightweight material made of fine threads of glass

modify (MOD-uh-fye)—to change; racing teams modify a car or engine in order to make it faster or more powerful.

nitromethane (nye-tro-MEH-thane)—a mix of nitric acid and propane gas used as fuel in some dragsters

spoiler (SPOIL-uhr)—a winglike feature attached to the front of a car; spoilers help to keep dragsters steady on the track.

To Learn More

Cook, Nick. *The World's Fastest Cars.* Built for Speed. Mankato, Minn.: Capstone High-Interest Books, 2001.

Hintz, Martin, and Kate Hintz. *Top Fuel Drag Racing.* Drag Racing. Mankato, Minn.: Capstone Books, 1996.

Sessler, Peter C., and Nilda Sessler. *Drag Cars.* Off to the Races. Vero Beach, Fla.: Rourke Press, 1999.

Useful Addresses

Canadian Motorcycle Drag Racing Association
P.O. Box 93082
Langley, BC V3A 8H2
Canada

Museum of Drag Racing
13700 SW 16th Avenue
Ocala, FL 34473

National Hot Rod Association
2035 Financial Way
Glendora, CA 91741

Internet Sites

International Hot Rod Association
http://www.ihra.com

National Hot Rod Association
http://www.nhra.com

NHRA Junior Drag Racing League
http://www.nhra.com/junior/index.html

Index